978-1-912328-89-5

Published by Orla Kelly Publishing.

Orla Kelly Publishing
27 Kilbrody
Mount Oval
Rochestown
Cork
Ireland

Hello!

My goodness! I don't think anyone will be sad to see the last of 2020! It certainly has been a year like no other. Covid-19 swept across every corner of our world and changed the way we live, work and do business.

The way people purchase goods and services has changed. According to Josh Martin ONS, it took 7 years for online shopping to get from 9% to 19% of retail sales in the UK, but only four months to get from 19% to 33% in May 2020. Argos reported that its click and collect service increased by 32% and home delivery sales grew by 87% while its 573 stores were closed. Dixons PC World also reported that online sales recovered about two-thirds of lost store sales.

With the risk of Covid-19 ever present, I predict the move towards online shopping will continue in 2021. Consumers will research online before making cautious instore visits, click and collect will also continue to grow in popularity and home deliveries will be the only option for many including those cocooning. Businesses that adapt will be more successful than those that do not. Our world has changed, and we must change with it.

Social media marketing is not just a box ticking exercise! It is not a "nice to have", it is not just about engagement and networking, it is about using sophisticated advertising techniques to build brand awareness and generate sales. This diary will help you use social media more strategically. I help companies use social media to grow their businesses. I have trained more than 16,000 people over the last ten years, including 8,000 online students in the last 12 months. I am a social media author, coach and keynote speaker. My passion is helping individuals, businesses and organisations
to reach their full potential while teaching them to recognise their worth, differentiate themselves from their competitors and use social media more effectively and efficiently.

This planner is a useful resource to guide you through the practical process of creating and

implementing a social media strategy. All the topics discussed in this diary are explored more deeply, with accompanying webinars, video tutorials and down-loadable PDFs via my SellOnSocial.Media online training platform. Join my Social Media Academy to gain access to over 93 video training tutorials covering Facebook and Instagram marketing and paid advertising, live monthly training and coaching as well as discounts on one to one coaching packages.

To your success,

Louise

Personal Details

Name :

Address :

Telephone :

Email :

In Case of Emergency Please Contact

Name :

Address :

Telephone :

Email :

Passwords

Brand Colours

Notes

Social Media Channels 11

Table of Contents

Social Media Channels

Facebook

About

Set up in 2004, Facebook provides a platform for users around the world to connect with friends, family, communities and businesses. It is also the biggest social networking site based on global reach and active users.

Users

2.7 billion active users.

Demographics

54% female and 46% male.

Business

One of the most powerful social media platforms available to small businesses. Over 90 millions sme's are using Facebook as a marketing tool.

Facebook Business Page

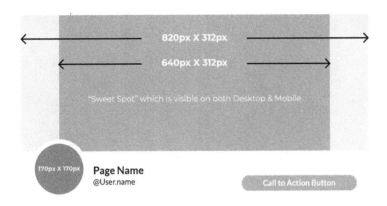

Profile Picture Size

170px x 170px
Use the company logo or a professional headshot (for sole traders)

Cover Photo Size

Displays at 820 pixels wide by 312 pixels tall on your page on computers and 640 pixels wide by 360 pixels tall on smartphones.

Cover Video

The recommended specification for videos covers are:

a. Cover video size: 828px by 315px
b. Cover video length: Between 20 and 90 seconds
c. Cover video must have a resolution of 1080p
d. Keep any text central

Page Name

75 characters.
Use your company name – aim for consistency with your website and other social media channels.

Username Limit

50 characters.
Aim for consistency with other social media channels.

Description Limit

155 characters.
Remember to communicate your unique selling proposition here. Why should a prospective customer do business with you?

Post Limit

63,206 characters.

Facebook Group

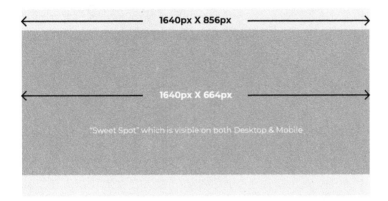

1640px X 856px

1640px X 664px

"Sweet Spot" which is visible on both Desktop & Mobile

Facebook Event Page

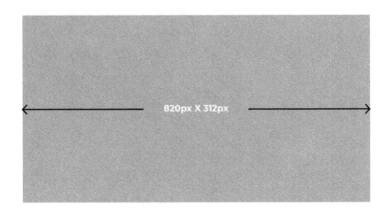

820px X 312px

Instagram

About

Launched in 2010, Instagram allows users to share videos and pictures with their audience.

Users

2.7 billion active users.

Demographics

54% female and 46% male.

Business

25 million businesses use Instagram.
Over 200 million users visit at least one business profile a day.
70% of shoppers look to Instagram for product discovery.

Trends for 2021

Instagram reels (Similar to Tiktok)
Augmented reality story filters.
Shopping directly on the platform.

Profile Picture Size	110 px x 110 px. Use the company logo or a professional headshot (for sole traders).
Username Limit	30 characters. Aim for consistency across other social media platforms.
Biography Limit	150 characters. Explain why people should follow your account and what they can expect. Why should potential customers do business with you? Use emojis to brighten up your bio!
Post Caption Limit	2200 characters.
Square Newsfeed Photo	1080px x 1080px.
Instagram Stories	1080px x 1920px.

Twitter

About

Founded in 2006, Twitter is a 'microblogging' platform that allows users to send and receive short posts called tweets. It is estimated that 500 million tweets are sent daily.

Users

330 million.

Demographics

34% female and 66% male.

Business

67% of B2B businesses are using Twitter as a marketing tool. 77% of Twitter users have a better impression of a brand when they respond to a tweet.

Twitter Business Profile

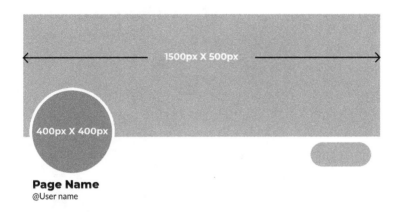

Page Name
@User name

Cover Photo Size (Header)	1500 px x 1500 px.
Profile Picture Size (Icon)	400 x 400px Use the company logo or a professional headshot (for sole traders).
Username Limit	15 characters. Aim for consistency across other social media platforms.

Biography Limit   160 characters.
Explain why people should follow your account and what they can expect. Include a company hashtag if you have one.

Tweet Limit   280 characters.

LinkedIn

About

LinkedIn was set up in 2003 to allow users to network with other professionals and further develop their careers and reputations.

Users

675 million.

Demographics

43% female and 57% male.

Business

LinkedIn is the number one social networking site that B2B marketers use to distrib-ute content.

LinkedIn Personal Profile

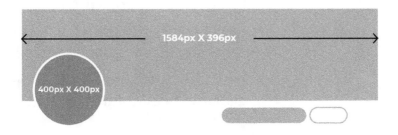

Profile Picture Size	400 px x 400 px.
Cover Image	1584 px x 396 px.
Profile Name	Your name (and maiden name if relevant)
Headline	120 characters including spaces. Has a really prominent position on your profile and is used to index your profile for relevant searches.
Summary	2000 characters that have a very prominent position. Strikes a balance between being general enough to cover your bases and specific enough to show up on search engines. Include keyword phrases – reinforce what is in your headline. On desktop the first 220 characters are immediately visible, with the rest requiring a user click on "View More".

On mobile the first 92 characters are immediately visible.

LinkedIn Company Page

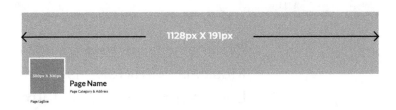

Profile Image 300 px x 300px.

Cover Image Size 1128 px x 191 px.

Page Tagline 120 Characters.
Explain why people should follow your business page. What makes your business different from others. What can you say to stand out.

Company Name 100 characters.

Company Description 2000 characters.

Status Update Limit	700 characters.

TikTok

About	Originally launched in 2014 as Musical.ly, TikTok is quickly becoming a popular form of user-generated content. Users can create, share and discover short videos such as singing, dancing and comedy content.
Users	800 million.
Demographics	44% female and 56% male.
Business	In June of 2020, TikTok announced its extended platform 'TikTok for business' that allows businesses to market and push branding on the site. Users spend an average of 52 minutes per day on the app.

Profile Picture Size	100 px x 100 px.
Video Size	1080 px x 1920 px.
Username Limit	24 characters.
Caption Limit	150 characters including hashtags.

YouTube

About

YouTube was founded in 2005 and has since seen 50 million users create, upload and share original video content. The platform also allows users to create their own profile, comment on other videos and subscribe to their favourite YouTubers.

Users

2 billion.

Demographics

32% female and 68% male.

YouTube Channel

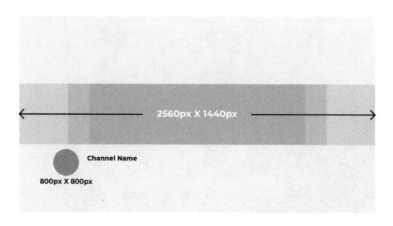

2560px X 1440px

Channel Name

800px X 800px

Profile Picture Size	800 px x 800 px.
Channel Cover Image	2560 px x 1440 px.
Username Limit	20 characters.
Channel description	1000 characters.
Video Title Limit	100 characters.
Video Description Limit	5000 characters.

Pinterest

About

Pinterest was set up in 2010 and is described as being a visual discovery engine that allows users to search for ideas and inspiration.

Users

416 million.

Demographics

71% female and 29% male.

Business

Pinterest is an excellent SEO (Search Engine Optimisation) tool. Increases brand awareness.

Profile Picture Size

160 px x 160 px.

Post Picture Size

600 px x 900 px.

Username Limit

30 characters.

Picture Description Limit

500 characters.

How to Create a Social Media Strategy

Fail to plan is a plan to fail!

Businesses that spend time planning their social media strategy are more successful. I meet so many businesses that literally create content on the go, run ads sporadically (or not at all) and then are frustrated with their results. If you are doing this, you are not using your time effectively, you are missing opportunities and you are more than likely spending good money after bad on social media ads.

Here is a very simple guide to help you plan your social media content and ads more effectively. I guarantee it will save you time and money. You will produce more effective, strategic content which will in turn enable you to run higher converting ad campaigns.

Step 1 – Set Your SMART Goals

The business goals you set for 2021 will greatly influence your social media content and ads. Failure to set goals often results in you wasting time and money on social media. If you do not know what you want to achieve you will simply meander along, with no purpose, direction and you may not make any

progress. Setting SMART Goals enables you to identify the starting and the finishing line. Goals keep you on track and accountable.

1. What are your business goals for 2021? Break these down by product/service/territory and also by month/quarter.
2. What are your social media goals for 2021?

2021 followers	Q1	Q2	Q3	Q4
Facebook				
Instagram				
Twitter				
LinkedIn				
Other				
Other				

3. Other metrics to tune into are
    a. Reach – the number of people seeing your social media posts on a weekly/monthly basis. Reach is a more important metric than followers as it is also an indication of how active your social media channels are as well as being a gauge of the quality of your content.

a. Reach – the number of people seeing your social media posts on a weekly/monthly basis. Reach is a more important metric than followers as it is also an indication of how active your social media channels are as well as being a gauge of the quality of your content.

b. Engagement – The way in which people are reacting to your social media content. People can engage by reacting/liking, commenting, sharing, clicking or viewing (a video). Engagement is directly related to the quality of your content.

Post engagements are like "votes" for your content. The more people engage (or vote) the more the algorithm (on whatever social media platform you are using) will show your content to a wider audience.

c. Enquiries – We market online but we sell offline (for the most part!) Having a goal around the number of enquiries generated from social media will encourage posts which will encourage people to reach out by direct message, email or other means.

d. Sales – Integrating a shop with your Facebook and Instagram channels as well as other online booking systems means that sales can be generated directly from social media.

e. Traffic to your website – set goals around driving traffic to your website from your social media channels.

Goals

Step 2 – Why Should Someone Do Business with You?

Do you know why customers choose your products/-services over your competitors? Often, when I ask this question, I get a look…. The look that says "of course I know!" But closer examination of websites, brochures, signage and other marketing tools tells a different story.

Developing a unique selling proposition (USP) for your company, products or services takes time and careful consideration. Once developed it must be used by everyone in the company as part of the marketing and sales strategy. It must be consistent, accurate and realistic.

So how do you uncover your USP?

1. Walk in Your Customers Shoes:

Write down all the reasons your customers choose to buy from you. What do they like about you? What need are you fulfilling? What problem are you solving? And why do they consistently choose you over your competitors? The answer may be relating to quality, location, convenience, reliability, customer service, cleanliness or availability. Remember, price is rarely the sole factor

why customers choose one product over another.
If you're unsure – ask them!

2. Understand What Motivates your Customers:

Go beyond your product features and think more of its benefits. What are the wider factors motivating your customers? What are the benefits to them? How are their lives or situation better from doing business with you?

3. Identify Why Customers Choose You Over Competitors:

Listen to customer feedback and encourage your staff to do likewise. Ask your best customers.

Once you have identified your USPs, make sure everyone in your organisation is clear on what they are. They should be used on all marketing material, on your website, in the descriptions on your social media channels, in your sales proposals and presentations. They should also be used to create a tag line that becomes closely associated with your business.

Complete the following sentences

The reasons you should do business with me/us is that . . . .

. . . .

I/We have expertise in . . . .

. . . .

I am/We are the only company that can . . . .

. . . .

My/Our promise to you is that . . . .

. . . .

I/We guarantee that you will benefit from . . . .

. . . .

I/We will make your life easier by . . . .

. . . .

Step 3: Customer Analysis and Profiling

Understanding your customers is the key to planning a social media campaign. It will enable you to identify key audiences, create content that will appeal to them and run more successful social media paid ad campaigns.

Customers are the lifeline of every business. Without customers there is no business. Businesses that understand their customers needs, wants and motivations have more of a chance of succeeding than those that do not. Businesses that understand their customers are better at product development, selecting distribution channels, pricing and marketing. In order to understand our customer, we need to ask ourselves the following questions :

- Who are our customers?
- What are their needs?
- Do I meet those needs?
- Are they satisfied with my product/service offering?
- How can I reach my customers?
  What will I say to them to encourage them to buy (more) from me?

1. Have a staff brain storming session

Here are some questions to consider as a group:

1. When people hear what you do, what question do they ask you?
2. What are the top questions you get asked all the time by your clients?
3. What does your ideal customer complain about?
4. What are the goals of your target audience?
5. What do they talk about continually?

2. Chat to at least 2/3 Customers

Here are some questions to consider using:

1. What do you like about us?
2. What bugs you about our business?
3. What might put you off coming in?
4. What can we do to make your life easier?

3. Create customer personas for all your customer groups

Use the information you have gathered from your research (brainstorming, customer chats, customer survey) along with the information from your Facebook Insights and Facebook Advertising Audience Insights to start creating your customer personas. If you feel out of your depth with Facebook Ads and Audiences, check out my "Six Step System to Success" to up your confidence and make your ads really work for you on www.sellonsocial.media.

Use the following questions to help you to create the profiles:

- Age
- Gender
- Where do they live?
- Where do they work?
- Do they work?
- What is going on in their lives?
- What do they worry about?
- What takes up their time?
- What do they do to de-stress?
- Where do they hang out?
- What do they read?

- What radio station do they listen to?
- What social networks do they use?
- What would make life easier?
- How can you make their lives easier?

Step 4: Creating a Content Plan

Understanding your customers is the key to successful content creation on Social Media, your website and in all your marketing materials. In the last section we investigated who our customers are. We also considered the reasons that they choose to do business with us. Having done some research into customer demo-graphics and psychographics we created customer personas. In this section we are going to start "having conversations" with our personas. We are going to visualize our typical customers and what we would say to them if they were sitting in front of us. Social media is about connecting with our audience and consistently communicating our core messages to them. You need to consider your social media chan-nels as a radio station where your customers can tune in. What would you broadcast to keep your listeners tuned in? Would you tune into a radio station where it broadcast one advertisement after another?.... What if the advertisements were not of great quality?.... I doubt you would

and your customers won't either..... If you use your social media channels to publish one advertisement after another your audience will tune out and they will stop engaging with your posts. If people stop interacting with your social media posts, it will have a negative impact on reach. The most important advice I can offer when it comes to creating

social media content is, it is not about what you want to say, it is about what your customer wants to hear about from you.

It is not about you. It is about them. If you publish content that is useful to your customer they are much more likely to engage.

Brand Awareness Content

Create engaging sociable content that your fans will interact with. It is not about selling it is about getting your brand in front of customers and potential cus-tomers. Brand impressions are the aim here – how many times someone sees your logo, brand colours etc. The quality of your content and how much it appeals to your audiences will determine how they engage with it (likes, comment, tag friends, share). Make your audience feel like they know you. This helps build trust.

Examples of awareness content include:

- Behind the scenes
- Out and out
- Business milestones
- Memes
- Throwback images, etc.

List at least 3 different examples of posts from behind the scenes in your business.

1.

2.

3.

List any business or industry milestones

1.

2.

3.

List any memes or inspirational quotes you can plan around key dates (see the Calendar at the back of this Planner for inspiration).

1.

2.

3.

Top Tip:

Feature you and your staff as much as possible in images and videos as this helps build brand awareness.

Consideration Content

This type of content enables your customers to connect with your brand in a more meaningful way. Consideration posts often offer advice or can be educational. How can you help your ideal customer right now? What advice can you give? Think about how you can position your company as an expert in the eyes of a potential customer.

List at least 3 different examples of posts that solve a problem for your customers:

1.

2.

3.

List at least 3 different examples of posts that offer tips/advice for your clients:

1.

2.

3.

Conversion or Sales Content

These are posts where you sell a product or service. Sales posts should have a clear call to action (call now, email here, PM my page etc.) and should be directed at your warmest audiences. Use paid ads to get sales posts in front of people that have previously visited your website, watched your social media video content and follow you on
Facebook & Instagram.

Notes

Advocate Content

This is content produced by your most loyal customers. It is really valuable content as potential customers are more likely to believe what people say about you rather than your own claims.

Encourage customers to post reviews/recommendations on your Facebook page. Set up a system to encourage as many reviews as possible. Hand pick people that you know will leave you a positive review. And... also ask for video reviews! You can use them as stand alone content or create a collage of multiple testimonials.

Encourage customers to post reviews/recommendations on your Facebook page.

Who will you ask to post a review on your Facebook page?

1.

2.

3.

Who will you ask to do a video testimonial?

1.

2.

3.

Facebook and Instagram Ads

Facebook Ads can be run across Facebook, Instagram and Messenger. They enable businesses both large and small to reach people that are most likely to become customers. Anyone who has a Facebook Business page or business Instagram account can use Facebook Ads. This offers small businesses the same opportunity as large multinationals. Businesses set their own budget and spend as much or as little as they wish. Facebook will guide you through the steps to optimise your budget.

Facebook offers us the opportunity to create different audiences for our ads. The audience is who we want Facebook to show our ads to. You can select a different audience for every ad including audiences using demographics or remarketing audiences.

Please list below "Custom" audiences that you can potentially create.

Examples of custom audiences include people that have been on your website, people on your mailing list, people who have spent time watching videos on Facebook and Instagram and people who have intereacted with your Facebbok page or Instagram business account.

Please list below "Lookalike" audiences that you can potentially create.

Lookalike audiences are cold audiences that "look like" any of your custom audiences.

What "Saved" audiences can you create?

Use your customer persona or avatar to create saved audiences based on demographics and interests.

Can you think of a lead magnet you can offer cold prospects?

Can you produce a simple ebook, cheat sheet, industry report - something that your ideal customer will value enough that they will provide you with their email address or phone number in exchange for what you are offering?

How can you keep the lines of communication open?

Can you email them, text them or use Facebook Ads to remarket to them? Use your warmest audiences here. Think also about Messenger ads.

What is the easiest way to draw in the warmest prospects?

Can you offer a free trial, a tester, a free consultation or a money back guarantee?

How can you convert the warmest prospects?

Once prospects have used their free trial/consultation etc – how can you get them to purchase? What conversion ads will you run?

Creating Ads That Convert

It is so important when creating your ad to choose your headline and ad description well.

- What will appeal to your target audience?
- How can you capture their attention?
- What is important and will resonate with your audience over the lifetime of your ad?
- What is the most important aspect of the ad that will be useful to your ideal customer?
- What problem are you solving? What need are you filling?
- Can you incentivise the reader to act quickly by offering an early bird offer or limited availability?
- Can you add credibility by including examples of awards, accolades or social proof?
- Use local town names if relevant
- Use month references too if relevant
- It is always advisable to include a "call to action" button – This tells the reader what you want them to do next (call now, email now, shop now etc.).
- Remember to sell benefits not just features.

Creating Your Ad Text

Remember to capture attention in the first five words. Tell your audience what problem you are solving. What social proof can you offer? How can you incentivise your targets to act sooner rather than later?

Reviewing Ad Performance

It is possible to see a breakdown of how each ad is performing in terms of its result, reach, cost and relevance score through Facebook.

Reach   The number of people that saw your ad.

Impressions   The number of times your ad was viewed.

Cost   The average cost you paid for each action or result (the action related to the campaign objective. For example, if the campaign objective is to grow page likes, the action is the number of new page likes)

Budget   The amount you are willing to pay for each ad set.

Clicks   Clicks on the ad.

CTR Click through rate (clicks/impressions).

CPC Cost per click.

For more detail visit www.SellOnSocial.Media and view my course on "Measuring the Success of Facebook and Instagram ads".

Content Calendar - Get Real About 2021

This space is for planning your year in themes, concepts and seasons – use the prompts or come up with your own!

Q1	January	February	March
You have lots of options – choose a seasonal or monthly or even annual theme as an anchor for your marketing efforts.	Make 2021 your year - create posts that discuss you and your customers' resolutions, plans, commitments.	What is a rising trend for 2021 in your industry? Position yourself as an expert and pass your knowledge on to your followers.	What is your company core messages? Share these with your customers in a series of posts.

Q2	April	May	June
What is important to your business and customers?	Try out some new business tools & show the results to your clients over a period of time.	Choose a month to boost your followers or email list – run a BIG competition or create a lead magnet to draw people in.	AMA – Ask Me Anything month. Customers can text, email, message or comment with questions, and you answer as many as possible.

Q3

As you get used to using these tools, you will save time and feel more confident.

July

Share your space – work with another business or influential individual to cross-promote and bring a breath of fresh air to your social media presence.

August

User-generated content – get your superfans and long-term clients to leave reviews or give testimonials for your website.

September

Introduce your team – tell your customers about your staff or yourself. Show your human side!

Q4

Find more information and help at www. sellonsocial. media

October

This is the time to start sowing the seeds for Christmas – showcase your products or services, launch a new package or bundle.

November

Start thinking about your vision for 2022! Research what is coming next and start talking to your customers about it.

December

Tis the season! Offer maximum support to your customers because even if you are not affected by Xmas sales – they will be under pressure!

January 2021 Veganuary #Veganuary
Dry January #Dry January

01 Jan	New Year's Day	
02 Jan	National Buffet Day	#BuffetDay
03 Jan	Festival of Sleep Day	#FestivalOfSleepDay
04 Jan	National Trivia Day World Braille Day	#NationalTriviaDay #WorldBrailleDay
05 Jan	National Whipped Clean Day	#NationalWhippedCleanDay
06 Jan	National Bean Day	#NationalBeanDay
07 Jan	-	-
08 Jan	National Bubble Bath Day	#NationalBubbleBathDay

09 Jan	National Apricot Day	#NationalApricotDay
10 Jan	-	-
11 Jan	National Human Trafficking Awareness Day	#WearBlueDay (wear blue is the awareness campaign)
12 Jan	National Pharmacist Day	#nationalpharmacistday
13 Jan	National Sticker Day	#NationalStickerDay
14 Jan	-	-
15 Jan	National Hat Day	#NationalHatDay
16 Jan	-	-
17 Jan	World Snow Day World Religion Day	#snowday #WorldRegionDay

18 Jan	Martin Luther King Day	#MLKDay
19 Jan	-	-
20 Jan	National Penguin Day	#NationalPenguinDay
21 Jan	National Hugging Day	#NationalHuggingDay
22 Jan	Celebration of Life Day	#CelebrationofLifeDay
23 Jan	National Handwriting Day	#NationalHandwritingDay
24 Jan	National Compliment Day	#NationalComplimentDay
25 Jan	Opposite Day National Irish Coffee Day	#OppositeDay #NationalIrishCoffeeDay
26 Jan	National Spouse Day	#NationalSpouseDay

27 Jan	Holocaust Memorial Day	#HolocaustMemorialDay
28 Jan	Data Privacy Day	#PrivacyAware
29 Jan	National Puzzle Day	#NationalPuzzleDay
30 Jan	National Croissant Day	#NationalCroissantDay
31 Jan	National Hot Chocolate Day	#NationalHotChocolate Day

January 2021

Sun	Mon	Tue	Wed	Thu	Fri	Sat
					01	02
03	04	05	06	07	08	09
10	11	12	13	14	15	16
17	18	19	20	21	22	23
24	25	26	27	28	29	30
31						

January 2021   Week 1

MON

04

TUE

05

WED

06

January 2021   **Week 1**

| THU | |
| 07 | |

| FRI | |
| 08 | |

| SAT | |
| 09 | |

| SUN | |
| 10 | |

January 2021   Week 2

MON

11

TUE

12

WED

13

January 2021

THU 14	
FRI 15	
SAT 16	
SUN 17	

January 2021   **Week 3**

MON

18

TUE

19

WED

20

January 2021

Week 3

THU

21

FRI

22

SAT

23

SUN

24

MON	
25	

TUE	
26	

WED	
27	

January 2021   Week 4

| THU | |
| 28 | |

| FRI | |
| 29 | |

| SAT | |
| 30 | |

| SUN | |
| 31 | |

January 2021

What Worked This Month?

Most Successful Post

Most Successful Ad

What Accounts Have Most Inspired Me?

February 2021

Black History Month

#BlackHistoryMonth

Date	Black History Month	#BlackHistoryMonth
01 Feb	National Freedom Day	#NationalFreedomDay
02 Feb	Groundhog Day World Wetlands Day	#GroundhogDay #WorldWetlandsDay
03 Feb	National Golden Retriever Day	#NationalGoldenRetriever Day
04 Feb	World Cancer Day	#WorldCancerDay #WeCanICan
05 Feb	World Nutella Day	#WorldNutellaDay
06 Feb	-	-
07 Feb	Super Bowl LV	#SBLV
08 Feb	-	-

09 Feb	National Pizza Day	#NationalPizzaDay
10 Feb	Nation Umbrella Day	#NationUmbrellaDay
11 Feb	World Day of the Sick	#WorldDayOfTheSick
12 Feb	Chinese New Year	#ChineseNewYear #YearOfTheOx
13 Feb	World Radio Day	#WorldRadioDay
14 Feb	Valentine's Day	#ValentinesDay
15 Feb	Presidents' Day	#PresidentsDay
16 Feb	Pancake Tuesday	#PancakeTuesday
17 Feb	Random Acts of Kindness Day	#RandomActsOfKindness Day #RAKDay

18 Feb	National Drink Wine Day	#NationalDrinkWineDay
19 Feb	-	-
20 Feb	World Day of Social Justice National Love Your Pet Day	#SocialJusticeDay #LoveYourPetDay
21 Feb	International Mother Language Day	#MotherLanguageDay
22 Feb	National Margarita Day	#NationalMargaritaDay
23 Feb	National Banana Bread Day	#NationalBananaBreadDay
24 Feb	National Tortilla Chip Day	#NationalTortillaChipDay
25 Feb	National Toast Day	#NationalToastDay
26 Feb	National Pistachio Day	#NationalPistachioDay

27 Feb	International Polar Bear Day	#InternationalPolarBear Day
28 Feb	Golden Globe Awards	#GoldenGlobes

February 2021

Sun	Mon	Tue	Wed	Thu	Fri	Sat
	01	02	03	04	05	06
07	08	09	10	11	12	13
14	15	16	17	18	19	20
21	22	23	24	25	26	27
28						

February 2021   **Week 5**

MON	
01	

TUE	
02	

WED	
03	

February 2021

Week 5

THU
04

FRI
05

SAT
06

SUN
07

February 2021

MON	
08	

TUE	
09	

WED	
10	

February 2021

THU

11

FRI

12

SAT

13

SUN

14

February 2021   Week 7

MON	
15	

TUE	
16	

WED	
17	

February 2021   Week 7

| THU | |
| 18 | |

| FRI | |
| 19 | |

| SAT | |
| 20 | |

| SUN | |
| 21 | |

February 2021   Week 8

MON	
22	

TUE	
23	

WED	
24	

February 2021   Week 8

THU

25

FRI

26

SAT

27

SUN

28

February 2021

What Worked This Month?

Most Successful Post

Most Successful Ad

What Accounts Have Most Inspired Me?

March 2021	Women's History Month	#WomensHistory Month
01 Mar	Self-Injury Awareness Day	#SIAD
02 Mar	National Old Stuff Day	#NationalOldStuffDay
03 Mar	World Wildlife Day	#WorldWildlifeDay
04 Mar	National Grammar Day	#NationalGrammarDay
05 Mar	Employee Appreciation Day	#EmployeeAppreciation Day
06 Mar	National Oreo Cookie Day	#NationalOreoCookieDay
07 Mar	National Be Heard Day	#NationalBeHeardDay
08 Mar	International Women's Day	#InternationalWomensDay #BeBoldForChange

09 Mar	-	-
10 Mar	National Pack Your Lunch Day	#PackYourLunchDay
11 Mar	World Kidney Day	#WorldKidneyDay
12 Mar	National Plant a Flower Day	#NationalPlantaFlowerDay
13 Mar	National Good Samaritan Day	#GoodSamaritanDay
14 Mar	UK and Ireland Mother's Day	#MothersDay
15 Mar	World Consumer Rights Day	#WorldConsumerRightsDay
16 Mar	World Social Work Day	#WorldSocialWorkDay
17 Mar	Saint Patrick's Day	#StPatricksDay

18 Mar	Global Recycling Day	#GlobalRecyclingDay
19 Mar	National Poultry Day	#NationalPoultryDay
20 Mar	International Day of Happiness First Day of Spring	#InternationalDayOfHappiness #FirstDayOfSpring
21 Mar	World Down Syndrome Day	#WDSD #WorldDownSyndromeDay
22 Mar	World Water Day	#WorldWaterDay
23 Mar	World Meteorological Day National Puppy Day	#WorldMeteorologicalDay #NationalPuppyDay
24 Mar	World Tuberculosis Day	#WorldTuberculosisDay
25 Mar	International Waffle Day	#InternationalWaffleDay
26 Mar	National Spinach Day	#NationalSpinachDay

27 Mar	World Theatre Day	#InternationalWaffleDay
28 Mar	Respect Your Cat Day	#RespectYourCatDay
29 Mar	-	-
30 Mar	Take a Walk in the Park Day	#TakeAWalkInTheParkDay

March 2021

Sun	Mon	Tue	Wed	Thu	Fri	Sat
	01	02	03	04	05	06
07	08	09	10	11	12	13
14	15	16	17	18	19	20
21	22	23	24	25	26	27
28	29	30	31			

March 2021

MON	
01	

TUE	
02	

WED	
03	

LouiseMcDonnell

THU	
04	
FRI	
05	
SAT	
06	
SUN	
07	

March 2021

Week 10

MON	
08	
TUE	
09	
WED	
10	

March 2021   **Week 10**

| THU | |
| 11 | |

| FRI | |
| 12 | |

| SAT | |
| 13 | |

| SUN | |
| 14 | |

March 2021 **Week 11**

MON	
15	

TUE	
16	

WED	
17	

March 2021   **Week 11**

THU
18

FRI
19

SAT
20

SUN
21

March 2021

Week 12

MON	
22	

TUE	
23	

WED	
24	

March 2021

THU	
25	
FRI	
26	
SAT	
27	
SUN	
28	

March 2021

MON	
29	

TUE	
30	

WED	
31	

March 2021

What Worked This Month?

Most Successful Post

Most Successful Ad

What Accounts Have Most Inspired Me?

April 2021	Autism Awareness Month	#AutismAwareness Month
01 Apr	April Fool's Day	#AprilFoolsDay
02 Apr	World Autism Awareness Day Good Friday	#WorldAutismAwareness Day #GoodFriday
03 Apr	National Find a Rainbow Day	#NationalFindARainbow Day
04 Apr	Easter Sunday	#EasterSunday
05 Apr	-	-
06 Apr	International Day of Sport for Development and Peace	#IDSDP #WhiteCard
07 Apr	World Health Day	#WorldHealthDay
08 Apr	National Zoo Lovers Day	#NationalZooLoversDay

09 Apr	National Unicorn Day	#NationalUnicornDay
10 Apr	National Siblings Day	#NationalSiblingsDay
11 Apr	National Pet Day	#NationalPetDay
12 Apr	National Grilled Cheese Day International Day of Human Space Fight	#NationalGrilledCheeseDay #HumanSpaceFlight
13 Apr	-	-
14 Apr	National Dolphin Day	#NationalDolphinDay
15 Apr	National High Five Day World Art Day	#NationalHighFiveDay #WorldArtDay
16 Apr	National Wear Your Pajamas to Work Day	#PJDay
17 Apr	Husband Appreciation Day	#HusbandAppreciation Day

18 Apr	-	-
19 Apr	Bicycle Day	#BicycleDay
20 Apr	-	-
21 Apr	World Creativity and Innovation Day	#WorldCreativityAndInnovationDay
22 Apr	Earth Day	#EarthDay
23 Apr	World Book Day	#WorldBookDay
24 Apr	-	-
25 Apr	The 93rd Academic Awards (The Oscars)	#AcademyAwards
26 Apr	International Chernobyl Disaster Remembrance Day	#ChernobylDisasterDay

27 Apr	National Tell A Story Day	#NationalTellAStoryDay
28 Apr	World Day for Safety and Health at Work	#SafetyAndHealthAtWork
29 Apr	International Dance Day	#InternationalDanceDay
30 Apr	International Jazz Day	#InternationalJazzDay

April 2021

Sun	Mon	Tue	Wed	Thu	Fri	Sat
				01	02	03
04	05	06	07	08	09	10
11	12	13	14	15	16	17
18	19	20	21	22	23	24
25	26	27	28	29	30	

MON

29

TUE

30

WED

31

April 2021

THU

01

FRI

02

SAT

03

SUN

04

April 2021

MON

05

TUE

06

WED

07

April 2021 **Week 14**

| THU | |
| 08 | |

| FRI | |
| 09 | |

| SAT | |
| 10 | |

| SUN | |
| 11 | |

April 2021

MON	
12	
TUE	
13	
WED	
14	

April 2021

Week 15

THU

15

FRI

16

SAT

17

SUN

18

April 2021   Week 16

MON
19

TUE
20

WED
21

April 2021

Week 16

THU

22

FRI

23

SAT

24

SUN

25

April 2021

MON	
26	
TUE	
27	
WED	
28	

April/May 2021   Week 17

THU

29

FRI

30

SAT

01

SUN

02

April 2021

What Worked This Month?

Most Successful Post

Most Successful Ad

What Accounts Have Most Inspired Me?

May 2021

Cystic Fibrosis
Awareness Month

#CFAwareness

01 May	May Day World Lyme Day	#MayDay #WorldLymeDay
02 May	World Laughter Day	#WorldLaughterDay
03 May	World Press Freedom Day	#WorldPressFreedomDay
04 May	Star Wars Day World Asthma Day	#StarWarsDay #MayThe4thBeWithYou #WorldAsthmaDay
05 May	Cinco De Mayo	#CincoDeMayo
06 May	National No Diet Day	#NationalNoDietDay
07 May	World Password Day	#WorldPasswordDay
08 May	World Fair Trade Day	#WorldFairTradeDay

09 May	U.S. Mother's Day	#MothersDay
10 May	National Clean Your Room Day	#CleanYourRoomDay
11 May	National Denim Day	#DenimDay
12 May	International Nurses Day	#NursesDay
13 May	International Hummus Day	#InternationalHummus Day
14 May	National Buttermilk Biscuit Day	#NationalButtermilkBiscuit Day
15 May	International Day of Families	#FamilyDay
16 May	International Day of Light	#DayOfLight
17 May	World Telecommunication and Information Society Day	#WTISD

18 May	-	-
19 May	-	-
20 May	World Bee Day	#WorldBeeDay
21 May	Bike to Work Day	#BikeToWorkDay
22 May	International Day for Biological Diversity	#BiologicalDiversity
23 May	World Turtle Day	#WorldTurtleDay
24 May	National Brother Day	#BrotherDay
25 May	National Wine Day	#NationalWineDay
26 May	National Paper Airplane Day	#NationalPaperAirplaneDay

27 May	-	-
28 May	International Burger Day	#InternationalBurgerDay
29 May	National Biscuit Day	#NationalBiscuitDay
30 May	World MS Day	#WorldMSDay
31 May	World No Tobacco Day	#NoTobaccoDay

May 2021

Sun	Mon	Tue	Wed	Thu	Fri	Sat
						01
02	03	04	05	06	07	08
09	10	11	12	13	14	15
16	17	18	19	20	21	22
23	24	25	26	27	28	29
30	31					

THU

29

FRI

30

SAT

01

SUN

02

May 2021   **Week 18**

MON	
03	

TUE	
04	

WED	
05	

May 2021 **Week 18**

THU
06

FRI
07

SAT
08

SUN
09

May 2021   **Week 19**

MON

10

TUE

11

WED

12

May 2021

THU	
13	
FRI	
14	
SAT	
15	
SUN	
16	

May 2021

MON	
17	

TUE	
18	

WED	
19	

May 2021 **Week 20**

THU	
20	

FRI	
21	

SAT	
22	

SUN	
23	

May 2021 Week 21

MON	
24	

TUE	
25	

WED	
26	

May 2021

Week 21

THU

27

FRI

28

SAT

29

SUN

30

May/June 2021   **Week 22**

MON	
31	

TUE	
01	

WED	
02	

May 2021

What Worked This Month?

Most Successful Post

Most Successful Ad

What Accounts Have Most Inspired Me?

June 2021

01 June	Global Day of Parents	#GlobalDayOfParents
02 June	Global Running Day	#GlobalRunningDay
03 June	National Egg Day	#NationalEggDay
04 June	National Donut Day	#NationalDonutDay
05 June	World Environment Day	#WorldEnvironmentDay
06 June	D-Day Anniversary	#DDay
07 June	World Food Safety Day	#WorldFoodSafetyDay
08 June	World Oceans Day National Best Friend Day	#WorldOceansDay #NationalBestfriendDay

09 June	-	-
10 June	National Donald Duck Day	#NationalDonaldDuckDay
11 June	-	-
12 June	World Day Against Child Labour	#AgainstChildLabour
13 June	International Albinism Awareness Day	#AlbinismAwarenessDay
14 June	World Blood Donor Day	#WorldBloodDonorDay
15 June	World Elder Abuse Awareness Day	#WorldElderAbuseAwarenessDay
16 June	Fresh Veggies Day	#FreshVeggiesDay
17 June	Eat Your Vegetables Day	#EatYourVegetablesDay

18 June	International Picnic Day	#InternationalPicnicDay
19 June	National Martini Day	#NationalMartiniDay
20 June	Irish Father's Day	#FathersDay
21 June	National Selfie Day	#NationalSelfieDay
22 June	World Rainforest Day	#WorldRainforestDay
23 June	United Nations Public Service Day	#UNPublicServiceDay
24 June	National Handshake Day	#NationalHandshakeDay
25 June	Take Your Dog to Work Day	#TakeYourDogToWorkDay
26 June	-	-

27 June	National Sunglasses Day Micro-, Small and Medium-Sized Enterprises Day	#NationalSunglassesDay #MSMEDay21
28 June	-	-
29 June	National Camera Day	#NationalCameraDay
30 June	Social Media Day	#SMDay

June 2021

Sun	Mon	Tue	Wed	Thu	Fri	Sat
		01	02	03	04	05
06	07	08	09	10	11	12
13	14	15	16	17	18	19
20	21	22	23	24	25	26
27	28	29	30			

May/June 2021   Week 22

MON	
31	

TUE	
01	

WED	
02	

June 2021

THU

03

FRI

04

SAT

05

SUN

06

June 2021

MON	
07	

TUE	
08	

WED	
09	

June 2021

Week 23

| THU | |
| 10 | |

| FRI | |
| 11 | |

| SAT | |
| 12 | |

| SUN | |
| 13 | |

June 2021

MON	
14	

TUE	
15	

WED	
16	

June 2021

THU

17

FRI

18

SAT

19

SUN

20

MON

21

TUE

22

WED

23

June 2021

Week 25

THU

24

FRI

25

SAT

26

SUN

27

June 2021

Week 26

MON

28

TUE

29

WED

30

June 2021

What Worked This Month?

Most Successful Post

Most Successful Ad

What Accounts Have Most Inspired Me?

July 2021

01 July	Canada Day	#CanadaDay
02 July	World UFO Day	#WorldUFODay
03 July	-	-
04 July	Independence Day	#IndependenceDay
05 July	-	-
06 July	International Kissing Day	#InternationalKissingDay
07 July	World Chocolate Day	#WorldChocolateDay
08 July	-	-

09 July	National Sugar Cookie Day	#NationalSugarCookie Day
10 July	National Pina Colada Day	#NationalPinaColadaDay
11 July	World Population Day	#WorldPopulationDay
12 July	National Pecan Pie Day	#NationalPecanPieDay
13 July	Cow Appreciation Day National French Fry Day	#CowAppreciationDay #NationalFrenchFryDay
14 July	Bastille Day National Mac and Cheese Day	#BastilleDay #MacAndCheeseDay
15 July	World Youth Skills Day	#WorldYouthSkillsDay
16 July	World Snake Day	#WorldSnakeDay
17 July	World Emoji Day	#WorldEmojiDay

18 July	Nelson Mandela International Day National Ice Cream Day	#MandelaDay #NationalIceCreamDay
19 July	-	-
20 July	National Moon Day	#MoonDay
21 July	National Hot Dog Day	#NationalHotDogDay
22 July	-	-
23 July	-	-
24 July	International Self Care Day	#SelfCareDay
25 July	National Wine And Cheese Day	#NationalWineAndCheese Day
26 July	-	-

27 July	-	-
28 July	-	-
29 July	National Lasagne Day National Intern Day	#NationalLasagneDay #NationalInternDay
30 July	International Friendship Day National Cheesecake Day	#InternationalFriendshipDay #CheesecakeDay
31 July	National Avocado Day	#NationalAvocadoDay

July 2021

Sun	Mon	Tue	Wed	Thu	Fri	Sat
				01	02	03
04	05	06	07	08	09	10
11	12	13	14	15	16	17
18	19	20	21	22	23	24
25	26	27	28	29	30	31

June/July 2021

MON	
28	
TUE	
29	
WED	
30	

July 2021

THU	
01	
FRI	
02	
SAT	
03	
SUN	
04	

July 2021   Week 27

MON	
05	

TUE	
06	

WED	
07	

July 2021   Week 27

THU

08

FRI

09

SAT

10

SUN

11

July 2021   **Week 28**

MON

12

TUE

13

WED

14

July 2021

THU	
15	
FRI	
16	
SAT	
17	
SUN	
18	

July 2021   Week 29

MON

19

TUE

20

WED

21

July 2021

THU

22

FRI

23

SAT

24

SUN

25

MON

26

TUE

27

WED

28

July/August 2021

Week 30

THU	
29	
FRI	
30	
SAT	
31	
SUN	
01	

July 2021

What Worked This Month?

Most Successful Post

Most Successful Ad

What Accounts Have Most Inspired Me?

August 2021

01 Aug	National Girlfriend Day National Sister Day World Wide Web Day	#NationalGirlfriendDay #NationalSisterDay #WorldWideWebDay
02 Aug	National Colouring Book Day	#NationalColouringBook Day
03 Aug	National Watermelon Day	#NationalWatermelonDay
04 Aug		
05 Aug	National Underwear Day	#NationalUnderwearDay
06 Aug	National Beer Day	#NationalBeerDay
07 Aug	National Lighthouse Day	#NationalLighthouseDay
08 Aug	International Cat Day	#InternationalCatDay

09 Aug	National Book Lovers Day	#NationalBookLoversDay
10 Aug	National Lazy Day	#NationalLazyDay
11 Aug	-	-
12 Aug	World Elephant Day International Youth Day	#WorldElephantDay #InternationalYouthDay
13 Aug	International Left-Handers Day	#InternationalLeftHandersDay
14 Aug	World Lizard Day	#WorldLizardDay
15 Aug	National Relaxation Day	#NationalRelaxationDay
16 Aug	National Tell a Joke Day	#NationalTellAJokeDay
17 Aug	National Non-Profit Day	#NationalNonProfitDay

18 Aug	World Daffodil Day	#WorldDaffodilDay
19 Aug	World Humanitarian Day	#WorldHumanitarianDay
20 Aug	-	-
21 Aug	Senior Citizens Day	#SeniorCitizensDay
22 Aug	#NationalToothFairyDay	#NationalToothFairyDay
23 Aug	-	-
24 Aug	International Strange Music Day	#InternationalStrangeMusic Day
25 Aug	Spain's Tomato Throwing Festival	#Tomatina
26 Aug	National Dog Day	#NationalDogDay

27 Aug	-	-
28 Aug	National Bow Tie Day	#NationalBowTieDay
29 Aug	-	-
30 Aug	National Beach Day	#NationalBeachDay
31 Aug	-	-

August 2021

Sun	Mon	Tue	Wed	Thu	Fri	Sat
01	02	03	04	05	06	07
08	09	10	11	12	13	14
15	16	17	18	19	20	21
22	23	24	25	26	27	28
29	30	31				

August 2021

MON 02	
TUE 03	
WED 04	

August 2021

THU	
05	
FRI	
06	
SAT	
07	
SUN	
08	

August 2021

MON	
09	

TUE	
10	

WED	
11	

August 2021

Week 32

THU

12

FRI

13

SAT

14

SUN

15

August 2021

MON	
16	

TUE	
17	

WED	
18	

August 2021   **Week 33**

THU

19

FRI

20

SAT

21

SUN

22

August 2021

Week 34

MON
23

TUE
24

WED
25

August 2021

THU	
26	
FRI	
27	
SAT	
28	
SUN	
29	

August/September 2021　　　　　　　　　　　　　**Week 35**

| MON | |
| 30 | |

| TUE | |
| 31 | |

| WED | |
| 01 | |

August 2021

What Worked This Month?

Most Successful Post

Most Successful Ad

What Accounts Have Most Inspired Me?

September 2021

01 Sep	-	-
02 Sep	World Coconut Day	#WorldCoconutDay
03 Sep	-	-
04 Sep	World Beard Day	#WorldBeardDay
05 Sep	International Day of Charity	#InternationalDayOf Charity
06 Sep	Read a Book Day	#ReadABookDay
07 Sep	-	-
08 Sep	International Literacy Day	#InternationalLiteracyDay

09 Sep	National Teddy Bear Day	#NationalTeddyBearDay
10 Sep	World Suicide Prevention Day	#WorldSuicidePrevention Day
11 Sep	National Day of Service and Remembrance	#PatriotsDay
12 Sep	National Grandparents Day U.S.	#NationalGrandparents Day
13 Sep	-	-
14 Sep	-	-
15 Sep	International Day of Democracy	#InternationalDayOf Democracy
16 Sep	International Day Of The Preservation Of The Ozone Layer	#PreserveTheOzoneLayer
17 Sep	International Country Music Day	#InternationalCountry MusicDay

18 Sep	Oktoberfest European Heritage Days	#Oktoberfest #EuropeanHeritageDays
19 Sep	International Talk Like a Pirate Day	#InternationalTalkLikeA PirateDay
20 Sep	National Pepperoni Pizza Day	#NationalPepperoniPizza Day
21 Sep	International Day of Peace	#PeaceDay
22 Sep	World Rhino Day	#WorldRhinoDay
23 Sep	International Day of Sign Languages	#InternationalDayOfSign Languages
24 Sep	Punctuation Day	#PunctuationDay
25 Sep	World Dream Day	#WorldDreamDay
26 Sep	-	-

27 Sep	World Tourism Day	#WorldTourismDay
28 Sep	World Rabies Day	#WorldRabiesDay
29 Sep	-	-
30 Sep	International Podcast Day	#InternationalPodcastDay

September 2021

Sun	Mon	Tue	Wed	Thu	Fri	Sat
			01	02	03	04
05	06	07	08	09	10	11
12	13	14	15	16	17	18
19	20	21	22	23	24	25
26	27	28	29	30		

August/September 2021

Week 35

MON	
30	
TUE	
31	
WED	
01	

September 2021

Week 35

THU	
02	

FRI	
03	

SAT	
04	

SUN	
05	

September 2021

Week 36

| MON | |
| 06 | |

| TUE | |
| 07 | |

| WED | |
| 08 | |

September 2021   Week 36

| THU |
| 09 |

| FRI |
| 10 |

| SAT |
| 11 |

| SUN |
| 12 |

September 2021

MON	
13	

TUE	
14	

WED	
15	

September 2021

THU

16

FRI

17

SAT

18

SUN

19

September 2021

Week 38

MON	
20	
TUE	
21	
WED	
22	

September 2021   Week 38

THU

23

FRI

24

SAT

25

SUN

26

September 2021

MON	
27	
TUE	
28	
WED	
29	

September/October 2021

Week 39

THU	
30	
FRI	
01	
SAT	
02	
SUN	
03	

September 2021

What Worked This Month?

Most Successful Post

Most Successful Ad

What Accounts Have Most Inspired Me?

October 2021	Breast Awareness Month	#BreastAwareness Month
01 Oct	World Vegetarian Day International Coffee Day	#WorldVegetarianDay #InternationalCoffeeDay
02 Oct	International Day of Non-Violence	#InternationalDayof Non-Violence
03 Oct	National Boyfriend Day National Grandparents Day U.K.	#NationalBoyfriendDay #NationalGrandparents Day
04 Oct	National Taco Day	#NationalTacoDay
05 Oct	World Teachers' Day	#WorldTeachersDay
06 Oct	International Walk to School Day Grandparents Day in Ireland	#WalkToSchoolDay #GrandparentsDay
07 Oct	-	-
08 Oct	World Octopus Day	#WorldOctopusDay

09 Oct	World Post Day	#WorldPostDay
10 Oct	World Mental Health Day	#WorldMentalHealthDay
11 Oct	International Day of The Girls	#InternationalDayof TheGirls
12 Oct	National Farmers Day	#NationalFarmersDay
13 Oct	National Train Your Brain Day	#TrainYourBrainDay
14 Oct	National Dessert Day	#DessertDay
15 Oct	Global Handwashing Day National Pug Day	#GlobalHandwashingDay #NationalPugDay
16 Oct	World Food Day Boss's Day	#WorldFoodDay #BossesDay
17 Oct	National Pasta Day	#NationalPastaDay

Date	Day	Hashtag
18 Oct	-	-
19 Oct	-	-
20 Oct	International Chefs Day	#InternationalChefsDay
21 Oct	International Day of The Nacho	#InternationalDayofThe Nacho
22 Oct	National Nut Day	#NationalNutDay
23 Oct	-	-
24 Oct	United Nations Day	#UnitedNationsDay
25 Oct	European Day of Justice International Artists Day	#EuropeanDayOfJustice #InternationalArtistsDay
26 Oct	National Pumpkin Day	#NationalPumpkinDay

27 Oct	National Black Cat Day	#NationalChocolateDay
28 Oct	-	-
29 Oct	World Stroke Day	#WorldStrokeDay
30 Oct	National Checklist Day	#ChecklistDay
31 Oct	Halloween	#Halloween

October 2021

Sun	Mon	Tue	Wed	Thu	Fri	Sat
					01	02
03	04	05	06	07	08	09
10	11	12	13	14	15	16
17	18	19	20	21	22	23
24	25	26	27	28	29	30
31						

THU
30

FRI
01

SAT
02

SUN
03

October 2021   Week 40

MON
04

TUE
05

WED
06

October 2021

THU 07	
FRI 08	
SAT 09	
SUN 10	

October 2021

MON

11

TUE

12

WED

13

October 2021   **Week 41**

| THU |
| 14 |

| FRI |
| 15 |

| SAT |
| 16 |

| SUN |
| 17 |

October 2021

Week 42

| MON | |
| 18 | |

| TUE | |
| 19 | |

| WED | |
| 20 | |

October 2021

THU 21	
FRI 22	
SAT 23	
SUN 24	

October 2021

Week 43

MON

25

TUE

26

WED

27

October 2021 Week 43

THU

28

FRI

29

SAT

30

SUN

31

October 2021

What Worked This Month?

Most Successful Post

Most Successful Ad

What Accounts Have Most Inspired Me?

November 2021	Men's Health Awareness	Month #Movember
01 Nov	National Author's Day	#NationalAuthorsDay
02 Nov	-	-
03 Nov	International Stress Awareness Day	#StressAwarenessDay
04 Nov	-	-
05 Nov	American Football Day	#AmericanFootballDay
06 Nov	National Saxophone Day	#NationalSaxophoneDay
07 Nov	-	-
08 Nov	National Cappuccino Day	#NationalCappuccinoDay

09 Nov	-	-
10 Nov	World Science Day for Peace and Development	#WorldScienceDay #WSDPD
11 Nov	Veterans Day	#VeteransDay
12 Nov	World Pneumonia Day	#WorldPneumoniaDay
13 Nov	World Kindness Day	#WorldKindness Day
14 Nov	World Diabetes Day	#WorldDiabetesDay
15 Nov	Clean Out Your Fridge Day	#CleanYourFridge
16 Nov	-	-
17 Nov	National Take a Hike Day	#TakeAHikeDay

18 Nov	World Philosophy Day	#WorldPhilosophyDay
19 Nov	International Men's Day	#InternationalMensDay
20 Nov	-	-
21 Nov	World Television Day World Hello Day	#TelevisionDay #WorldHelloDay
22 Nov	-	-
23 Nov	National Adoption Day	#NationalAdoptionDay
24 Nov	National Jukebox Day	#NationalJukeboxDay
25 Nov	Thanksgiving Day	#Thanksgiving
26 Nov	Black Friday	#BlackFriday

27 Nov	Small Business Saturday	#ShopSmall
28 Nov	National French Toast Day	#FrenchToastDay
29 Nov	Cyber Monday	#CyberMonday
30 Nov	Giving Tuesday	#GivingTuesday

November 2021

Sun	Mon	Tue	Wed	Thu	Fri	Sat
	01	02	03	04	05	06
07	08	09	10	11	12	13
14	15	16	17	18	19	20
21	22	23	24	25	26	27
28	29	30				

November 2021

MON	
01	

TUE	
02	

WED	
03	

November 2021

THU

04

FRI

05

SAT

06

SUN

07

November 2021   Week 45

MON
08

TUE
09

WED
10

November 2021   Week 45

| THU | |
| 11 | |

| FRI | |
| 12 | |

| SAT | |
| 13 | |

| SUN | |
| 14 | |

November 2021   Week 46

MON

15

TUE

16

WED

17

November 2021

THU	
18	
FRI	
19	
SAT	
20	
SUN	
21	

November 2021

MON

22

TUE

23

WED

24

November 2021

THU	
25	

FRI	
26	

SAT	
27	

SUN	
28	

November/December 2021   Week 48

| MON | |
| 29 | |

| TUE | |
| 30 | |

| WED | |
| 01 | |

November 2021

What Worked This Month?

Most Successful Post

Most Successful Ad

What Accounts Have Most Inspired Me?

December 2021

01 Dec	National Christmas Lights Day World AIDS Day	#NationalChristmasLightsDay #WorldAIDSDay #WAD2021
02 Dec	-	-
03 Dec	International Day of Persons with Disabilities	#IDPD
04 Dec	National Cookie Day	#NationalCookieDay
05 Dec	International Volunteer Day	#InternationalVolunteer Day
06 Dec	Saint Nicholas Day	#StNicholasDay
07 Dec	-	-
08 Dec	National Chocolate Brownie Day	#NationalChocolate BrownieDay

09 Dec	Christmas Card Day	#ChristmasCardDay
10 Dec	Human Rights Day	#HumanRightsDay
11 Dec	International Mountain Day	#InternationalMountain Day
12 Dec	Poinsettia Day	#PoinsettiaDay
13 Dec	National Cocoa Day	#NationalCocoaDay
14 Dec	-	-
15 Dec	-	-
16 Dec	-	-
17 Dec	National Maple Syrup Day	#MapleSyrupDay

18 Dec	International Migrants Day	#InternationalMigrants Day
19 Dec	-	-
20 Dec	International Human Solidarity Day	#HumanSolidarityDay
21 Dec	Crossword Puzzle Day	#CrosswordPuzzleDay
22 Dec	-	-
23 Dec	-	-
24 Dec	Christmas Eve	#ChristmasEve
25 Dec	Christmas Day	#MerryChristmas
26 Dec	Saint Stephen's Day	#StStephensDay #BoxingDay

27 Dec	National Fruitcake Day	#NationalFruitcakeDay
28 Dec	Card Playing Day	#CardPlayingDay
29 Dec	-	-
30 Dec	-	-
31 Dec	New Years Eve	#NYE

December 2021

Sun	Mon	Tue	Wed	Thu	Fri	Sat
			01	02	03	04
05	06	07	08	09	10	11
12	13	14	15	16	17	18
19	20	21	22	23	24	25
26	27	28	29	30	31	

November/December 2021

Week 48

MON	
29	

TUE	
30	

WED	
01	

December 2021

Week 48

THU 02	
FRI 03	
SAT 04	
SUN 05	

December 2021

MON	
06	

TUE	
07	

WED	
08	

December 2021   **Week 49**

THU
09

FRI
10

SAT
11

SUN
12

December 2021

Week 50

MON	
13	

TUE	
14	

WED	
15	

December 2021 Week 50

THU	
16	
FRI	
17	
SAT	
18	
SUN	
19	

December 2021   **Week 51**

MON

20

TUE

21

WED

22

December 2021   **Week 51**

| THU | |
| 23 | |

| FRI | |
| 24 | |

| SAT | |
| 25 | |

| SUN | |
| 26 | |

December 2021   **Week 52**

MON

27

TUE

28

WED

29

December 2021/January 2022

THU	
30	
FRI	
31	
SAT	
01	
SUN	
02	

December 2021

What Worked This Month?

Most Successful Post

Most Successful Ad

What Accounts Have Most Inspired Me?

2021 Social Media Content Masterclass

€99
Free

with this

COUPON
2021master

Go to
www.sellonsocial.media
/courses/2021

In this masterclass, Louise will take you through the steps you need to create a year-long content plan for your business. Learn about the five stages of the customer journey and how this relates to social media content and ads.

Social Media is undoubtedly one of the most power-ful tools we own to boost sales and foster business growth – but it's not enough. That's why I've spent years developing a system for publishing content that clears the fog to reveal quantifiable results in weeks, not months.

CPSIA information can be obtained
at www.ICGtesting.com
Printed in the USA
BVHW041953221220
596291BV00020B/661